GREG BIFFLE

Connor Dayton

TRADUCCIÓN AL ESPAÑOL:
Eduardo Alamán

J SP B BIFFLE, G. DAY
Dayton, Connor
Greg Biffle

PowerKiDS press & **Editorial Buenas Letras**™
New York

Published in 2008 by The Rosen Publishing Group, Inc.
29 East 21st Street, New York, NY 10010

First Edition

Editor: Jennifer Way
Book Design: Michael J. Flynn
Book Layout: Kate Laczynski and Lissette González
Photo Researcher: Nicole Pristash

Photo Credits: All photos © Getty Images.

Cataloging Data

Dayton, Connor.
  Greg Biffle / Connor Dayton; traducción al español: Eduardo Alamán. — 1st ed.
     p. cm. — (NASCAR champions)
  Includes bibliographical references and index.
  ISBN-13: 978-1-4042-7646-8 (library binding)
  ISBN-10: 1-4042-7646-7 (library binding)
  1. Biffle, Greg, 1969– —Juvenile literature. 2. Stock car drivers—United States—Biography—Juvenile
literature. 3. Spanish language materials. I. Title.

Manufactured in the United States of America

Web Sites: Due to the changing nature of Internet links, the Rosen Publishing Group, Inc., has developed an online list of Web sites related to the subject of this book. This site is updated regularly. Please use this link to access the list: www.powerkidslinks.com/nas/gbiff/

Contents

Contenido

Greg Biffle is a NASCAR driver. He was born on December 23, 1969. Biffle was born in Vancouver, Washington.

Greg Biffle es piloto de NASCAR. Biffle nació el 23 de diciembre de 1969, en Vancouver, Washington.

4

Biffle drives for the Roush Racing team. He lives in Mooresville, North Carolina. Mooresville is sometimes known as Race City, USA.

Biffle corre para el equipo Roush Racing. Biffle vive en Mooresville, Carolina del Norte. A Mooresville se le llama la Capital de Carreras de Autos de los Estados Unidos.

6

7

Biffle started out racing in NASCAR's Craftsman Truck **Series**. Biffle won that series' **Rookie** of the Year award in 1998.

Biffle comenzó a correr en NASCAR en la **serie** Craftsman Truck. En 1998, Biffle ganó el premio de **Novato** del Año.

8

9

In 2001, Biffle moved up to the Busch Series. Racers drive stock cars in this group of races. That year he won that series' Rookie of the Year award.

En 2001, Biffle pasó a la serie Busch. En esta serie se compite en autos *stock*. Biffle ganó el premio de Novato del Año.

11

Biffle did well in the Busch Series. He was the series **champion** in 2002. The best Busch Series drivers move up to the Nextel Cup Series.

A Biffle le fue muy bien en la serie Busch. En 2002, Biffle fue el **campeón** de esta serie. Los mejores pilotos de la serie Busch pasan a la serie Nextel.

12

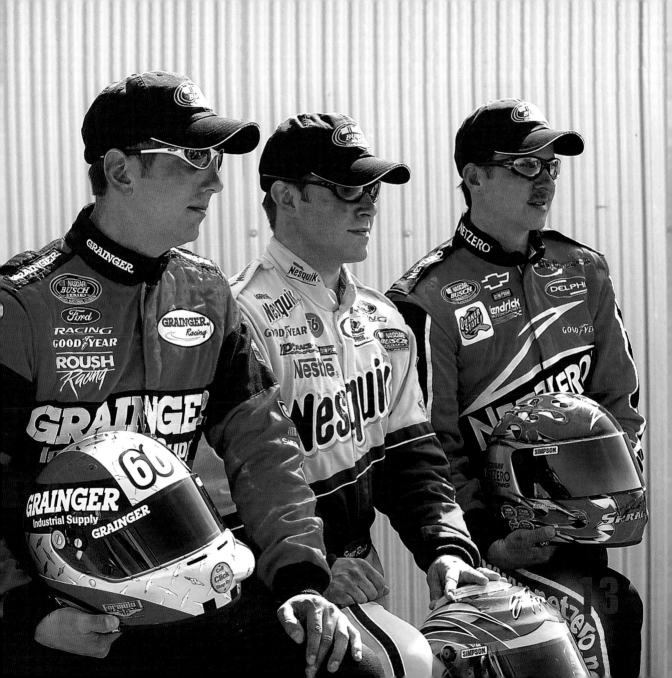

Biffle moved up to the Nextel Cup Series in 2003. Biffle worked hard to **improve** as a driver.

En 2003, Biffle pasó a la serie Nextel. Biffle tuvo que esforzarse mucho para **mejorar** como piloto.

14

Biffle races a Ford Fusion. His race number is 16. You can see the names of the Roush team's **sponsors** on the car.

Biffle corre en un Ford Fusion. Su número es el 16. Los nombres de los **patrocinadores** del equipo Roush están pintados en su auto.

17

When he is not racing, Biffle helps run the Greg Biffle **Foundation**. This is a **charity** that he set up to help take care of animals.

Cuando no está compitiendo, Biffle ayuda en la **Fundación** Greg Biffle. Esta es una institución de **beneficencia** que ayuda al cuidado de los animales.

18

Biffle is signed on to race on the Roush team until 2008. He hopes to keep improving and to remain a NASCAR champion.

Biffle correrá con el equipo Roush hasta 2008. Biffle espera seguir mejorando y seguir siendo un campeón de NASCAR.

Glossary

champion (CHAM-pee-un) The best, or the winner.

charity (CHER-uh-tee) A group that gives help to the needy.

foundation (fown-DAY-shun) A group set up to give help for a cause.

improve (im-PROOV) To get better.

rookie (RU-kee) A new player.

series (SIR-eez) A group of races.

sponsors (SPON-serz) People or groups that pay for someone else, such as a racer.

Books

Stevens, Josh. *Greg Biffle*. St. Louis: Reedy Press, 2006.

Kelley, K. C. *NASCAR: Racing to the Finish*. Pleasantville, NY: Reader's Digest Books, 2005.

22

Glosario

beneficencia (la) Un grupo que ayuda a los necesitados.

campeón(a) (el/la) Una persona que es la mejor, la ganadora.

fundación (la) Un grupo que ayuda a una causa.

mejorar Hacerse mejor.

novato (el/la) Una persona nueva en cierta actividad.

patrocinadores (los) Personas o grupos que pagan dinero para apoyar a una persona.

serie (la) Un grupo de carreras.

Libros en español

Doeden, Matt. *Autos de carrera / Stock Cars*. Capstone Press, 2007.

Kirkpatrick, Rob. *Dale Earnhardt Jr. Piloto de NASCAR*. PowerKids, Editorial Buenas Letras, 2002.

Index

Índice

24